MIRRAN THOUGHT

MIRRAN THOUGHT

Spitzwiesenstr. 50
90765 Fürth
Germany

www.dwmirran.de
www.empty.de
empty@empty.de

READ SEVENTEEN
(MT-600)

Printed by BOD
In de Tarpen 42
D-22848 Norderstedt
www.bod.de
info@bod.de

First printing 2018

MIRRAN THOUGHT is the publishing arm of
Mirran Threat, a company devoted to releasing the
music and writings of the various members of Doc
Wör Mirran. Mirran Thought and Mirran Threat are
both divisions of MT Undertainment.

Herstellung und Verlag:
BoD - Books on Demand, Norderstedt
ISBN 978-3-7460-7966-0

Chloride
And The Three Rivers

Joseph B. Raimond

Written and drawn in 2017:
Chloride, Arizona
Three Rivers, California
Las Vegas, Nevada
San Luis Obisbo, California
Monterey, California
San Francisco, California

Edited in Fürth, Germany

As always, in loving memory of Frank
Abendroth and Tom Murphy.

For Conny, my perfect angel

Dedicated to Eric Hysteric

This is DWM release Nr. 150

-Ugly Rumours-

Ugly rumours
Long since forgotten
Or explained
Checked out and
Never came back
They bought the album
Turned the trick
Then moved on
Like the roomers
Needles dangling
From their junk heavy arms
They shuffled away
Pushing their shopping carts
With not a second of fame
Walking the City streets
You might still
See one around

-Crumble-

Crumbling towards nirvana
Will I make it?
Or will I fall apart
In front of the finish line
Am I really one
Of the last generation
That must meet
Oblivion
On its terms?
And not on mine?
I want more of a future
In my future

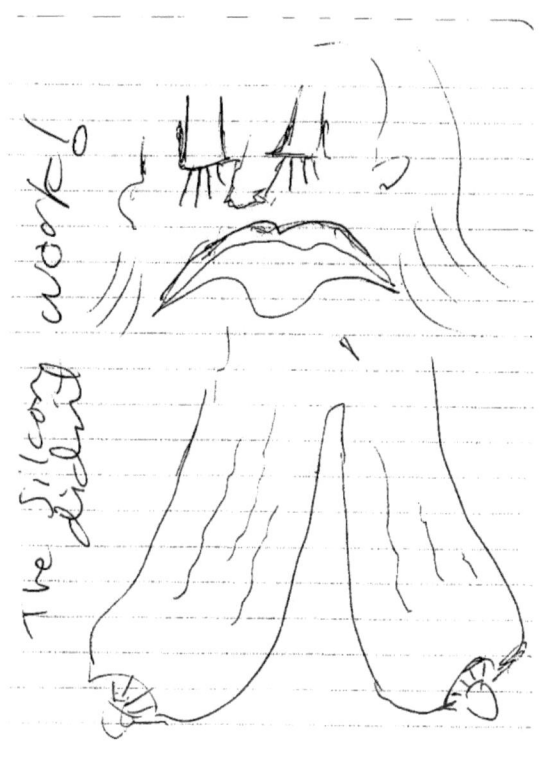

-Chloride-

In Chloride, Arizona
Phillis the chicken
Went missing
It'd been in the papers
If Chloride had a paper

I would have take the subway
If they'd had one, but
With only 352 population
They don't even
Have a bus

Don't go looking
For a hospital
A police station
Or a library
Either

(oops, they do have a library)

But hey!
They do have a train station
Or, should I say
Did
Looks like it was
Abandoned
Many decades ago

But still,
Better than nothing

I did see a pickup truck
Drive into town
Yesterday!

And the rains
Have put the hillsides
Into a wonderful
Poetic
Hue of green

But Chloride
Does have something
Few other places have:

Peace

Quiet

Where time is allowed,
No,
Almost forced

To
Stand still

Where one can pause
And take stock
Of one's life

And that is something
Chloride
Can be damn
Proud of

-Untitled-

Pussy whipped
He called me
My own father
He hated my sensitivity
He hated my "too European"
Upbringing

He hated me

Well,
Maybe not
But I know
He didn't
Love me enough

He loved his sorrow
Nurtured his guilt
And regret more
They were
His true children

-Untitled-

Down by the river
I didn't shoot
My baby

No,
I held her close
Whispered lovely
Whispers
For her ears only
And felt
That I had come home
Belonged, well
Somewhere

I felt good
Something
I'm not very good at

-*Wheelchair*-

The sun finally came out
But too late
The cold had already set
In our old bones

But still
We wandered
The wharf
Two of many
Badly dressed tourists

And we ate
Of the delicious
Clam chowder
Let ourselves
Be talked into buying a t-shirt

And leaving the wharf
I gave an old lady
Homeless
In a wheelchair
A fiver
And she smiled
The most wonderful
Honest smile

And I could finally
If just for a few minutes
Forgive myself
For being
Such an ugly tourist

-Blast-

Floating the one
Letting it land on two
Three tomorrow
Hey,
Let's just forget it
Altogether

Total freedom
Sounds in our heads
Sounds in our souls
Blasting the structure
Come with me

To freedom

-The City-

Back in the City
My city
A city filled with
Broken dreams
Some of them were mine

A city filled with
Hopelessness
Some of it was mine

The fallen
Pushing their worldly possessions
Around in the shopping carts
They stole from the Safeway
On Market and Church

More of the fallen
Wandering the streets
Aimless
Deep in discussions
With themselves

Oh, I escaped
Early enough
But never in my heart
The shopping cart I push
Is filled with guilt

-Three Rivers-

Three rivers
They call it
But we found five
And the water
All looks the same
While bathing us
It kisses the unworthy
The complaining
And with its buddy
This bottle of bourbon
Sitting next to me
Patiently waiting for me
To stop writing
Together, these
Best friend liquids
Help me write
This shit

-Tenderloin -

She said
I should
Give her
A hundred dollars
!

I told her
Hey, you give ME
A hundred dollars
She said
I looked like a
Millionaire
And she could tell
I still had all my
Original
Teeth

So, topped
I gave her all I had
At the time
A fiver
She thanked me
And said
Now she only got
Ninety-five
To go!

Hey honey!
Anything that
Happens
In Las Vegas
Stays
In Las Vegas.

-*Vegas*-

The real poverty
In this city
Of illuminated
Plastic
Is not begging
On the streets

No,
It is standing in the
Elevator
Wearing a
5 grand suit and tie
Or
Sitting in the back seat
Of the black stretch limo
Or
Throwing twenty-five dollar
Chips
To the silicon boobed
Bunny
Behind the blackjack
Table

-Omaha-

Born in the
Butthole of the world
I have every right
To be a gun toting
Cowboy hat wearing
Pickup truck driving
NRA card carrying
Country music listening
Republican voting
Redneck

Rise above!
I'm gonna
Rise above!

-Carsten-

He walked out
Through the in door
Pissed on the album cover
And was delighted
By the results

We all had a good laugh
Though, at his expense
As water woulda been
Just as good
And wouldn't have
Stank so much

As revenge
He prepared
Another of his dangerous
Cigarettes
Which blew up
In my naïve
And pimpled face

Still,
No one was cooler
Than us!

-Bro!-

Labeling me
A bleeding-heart liberal
Is only your weak attempt
At justifying
Your inability
To feel guilt
For your immoral actions
For your inability to care
For your lack of empathy

You've been studying
Pretty darn hard there
At Walmart University

-Untitled-

Let those dark shadows
Which, should they come to light
Promise the pain and horror
Their unpronounceable
Latin names imply

No, let them
Remain in their darkness
Their names not uttered
Let me bathe in the day's
Sunshine
But not transparent

Oblivious

when
At the age of fifty
My last argument
with my dad, likewise
I turned back
Into a sniveling
shit kid

Why couldn't
I tell him
to do...

FUCK!

-Untitled-

When a bird flies
Away
You thought, for
Forever
What do you do
When it wants back in?
Ignore it?
Roast it for lunch?
Let it hurt you again?
Let it pick out your
Eyes again?

-Fifty-Five And Ten-

At ten years old
I should have been outside
Playing
With my friend Jim

But that summer
All I wanted, All I
Could think about
Was killing myself

Oh, I admit
Not in such a concrete form
But;
I have since learned
At the age of almost
Fifty-five
To see the death wish
For what it is

All I know
Is that at ten
That summer
Night for night
I laid in bed
And cried

And during the day
When I should
Have been happy
Ready to go outside
And play with Jim
Well,
My childhood summer
Knew only darkness

At the age of ten
I learned
Bottomless sorrow
Came face to face
With that
Blackest of black
Gloom

-SFO-

This long,
Scary runway
Almost
A home away from home
How often
Have I roared through
Passed over
Its concrete planes
In, uh…..
Planes

Coming or going
But,
Always so nervous
Of falling
From your waiting
Beautiful blue skies

-Woodburn-

We moved to the village
While dad was in
Viet Nam

We, my sister and I
Recorded a cassette for him
All we could do though
Was laugh

Mom kissed him
When he got back
From the war
The only time I ever
Saw her kiss him

Me, racing a neighbor's boy
On our bikes
Me losing
And dad getting mad

Our old ugly neighbor
Threw away our new bikes
He hated children
Later,
He threw out my new shoes
That mom had just bought
And left out in the hall

Jumping off the ledge
With an umbrella
Thinking I would float
Gently to the ground

Mom getting mad
When the new building we
Had just moved into
Got all these
Ugly cracks in the walls

Getting lost
In my new school
In the scary hallways
On the first day of school
And the other children
Laughing

Waiting for the school bus
A woman,
Screaming
Came from a building
Carrying a baby
Who had just swallowed
A bottle of
Medication

Pissing in my pants
Walking home from school
Because the dirty, stinking
School toilets
Were so disgusting
I couldn't
Hold it anymore

My uncle
Coming to visit from Germany
For the first time
I thought hippies cool

Feeling so excited
When my dear
German grandma
Who I loved
More than anything else
In this world
Sent us a Christmas box

-Cannery-

Cannery row in Monterey,
California
Is a poem?
Still?
Was a poem, perhaps!
Is full of beautiful animals
Caged
Is full of ugly
Fat tourists
Is good food
Expensive
Is inspiration
Certainly
Is good air
Take a deep breath
Is a tourist trap
Get out your cameras
Is the best of America
Is the worst of America
Is money
To flaunt
Is sunshine
That gives life

-Tenderloined-

Trucks driving by
Cars honking
A police car wails through
The clogged traffic
Trying to spread

Workers, digging up the street
More workers, erecting new
Residential apartments

The street evangelists
Each with his megaphone
Or amplifier
Trying to out-yell
The other
With their versions of the verse
To a deaf, hurrying public
That doesn't care
And walks by
As quickly as they can

The endless numbers
Of the homeless
Street souls
America's dream
Turned nightmare
As they beg for change

Conny and I
Holding hands
As a man, smiling
Yells to us
"Love, American style!"

As the one American
Among us
Only I
Know what he is talking about

-Two-

Three
Is sometimes okay
The fourth, no way!
I prefer
To live
In two dimensions
Where color and form
Are timeless
Where,
Indeed time
Becomes meaningless

-Rolling Hills-

Virginia smiles
When my beloved
Grandma came to visit
With her German gifts
And chocolate

Bad boys honking
A horn in my ear
And my dad, cooking
French fries
Ran out and chased
Those boys away
Only to find,
Our kitchen on fire
He never cooked French fries again

Watching a little girl
Who lived in our building
Swinging her new little
Kitten
Around by the tail
And my mom getting
Angry at her

On the weekends,
Driving with daddy out to the bridge
To watch freight trains

Us all driving
Every Saturday
Out to meet mom on her lunch break
I always ate
A hotdog

Before he went off
To Viet Nam
Dad and I cutting a path
Through the woods
Behind our building
To the nearby corner store
We both got poison ivy
Real bad that time

Playing in the
"Little Woods"
In front of our building
Watching
Daddy-long-legs
Trying to hide
In the brickwork

Getting my finger slammed
In the car door
When my aunt Jean
Came to visit

Ripping off a toenail
On the sewing machine pedal
And then going to the hospital
And getting the biggest shot
The world had ever seen
Into my aching toe

Panic when mom brought
My sister and I to the dentist
It was never fair
My mouth
Full of cavities
My little sister
Never had even one
The nurses making fun of me
Calling me a "chicken"

Driving to the store
My first encounter
With hippies
As they spit on our car
As we drove by

Building a massive snow-fort
That took until spring
To finally melt

Dad finally
Getting sent off to
Viet Nam
Mom worrying about him
While he was out fucking
The Vietnamese whores

-Dean-

What,
This is where
James Dean died?
Really?

Never saw
One of his films
But still, somehow,
….cool….
To get a feeling
For this place
Of a famous death

Endless, endless
Green rolling hills
Beautiful,
Like a dream world

As I drive,
Up and down these green hills
It makes me wonder
Am I the lucky one
Or was he?

Three Rivers of Love

-437th-

There were only four Beatles
(well, six actually!)
And there are more than enough
Fifth Beatles around

Doing whatever I can
Friend of a friend
Who met John once

-or-

Being the "opening band"
Of the opening band
Of John Lennon's son's band

I figure,
That makes me
The 437th Beatle

I'll take
What I can get

-Proximity-

As close as I ever got
To being a street bum
Living in "the City"
I learned hunger
Living off
Margarine and white bread
Sandwiches for a week
Till payday

Mom learned hunger
As a child
In war-torn Germany
In the second world war

I learned hunger
As a student
In the war-torn debris
Of my mind

-Only Yesterday-

I woke up
To find myself
A diseased, old jerk
Someone I would have
Laughed at
Only yesterday

Only yesterday
Was really
About forty years ago
Before the curse
Of the disappearing
Decades
Shortened my life

While busy
Cursing this curse
If find myself
More diseased
Than
Ever
!

-Trumoeba-

Voting for the worst
Most lowly
Disgusting
Example of
Human life

My
Daddy
was
In
The
Service!

-Rain-

I have come
Travelled
Thousand
Thousand
Thousand
Thousand
Thousand
Thousand
Thousand
Thousand
Thousand
And then some
Friggin' kilometers
(don't know how many miles that is)
To the land
Of the eternal sun
And all I see is
Rain!

It never rains in
Southern California!?!
Who ever thought up
That shit?

I brought
The German rain
With me

-A Poem For Brian Ladd-

With my feet again
Touching down
On the sacred soil
I feel more and more
A stranger in my own land

A land that once
Not so long ago
Inspired and awed
Among the world's dreamers
The hopeful and enslaved
The fallen souls

Has the empire
Of compassion fallen
Where now "politics of pity"
Are the politics of fools
Of liberal mice
Not real men

But is it not this compassion
That you so mock
With your bad jokes
That defines this thing
We call humanity?

That brings us
Out of the realm
Of mice
And into that of real men?

Is it not the humanity in my heart
That defines our concept
Of compassion?
Of empathy?

Does this not make me a
"Real man"?
And is this not what your
"America"
Has always stood for?

If so, well
Brian
You really suck
At being an American

-Guts-

When the rain
Came
So did
The slugs
And icky snails
By the hundreds,
No, thousands
To bask in the
Steamy sunshine
Of the wet
Bicycle path

And then
SHE came
The cyclist
The snail and slug
Grim reaper
As she sped
Along the path
Running over
The slimy beings
Splat,
Splat!
Her back
Mountain bike tire
Kicking
The slimy guts

Of the poor
Snail and slug
Victims
Onto her back

As she cycled by
I turned and saw
Her back was full of the
Slime and guts
Of the snail and slug
Souls

-Round-

Of course,
The world is round
But so are my thoughts
My emotions
They're
Always going round
And round
And round
And round

It is such a short
Easy step
From the light of joy
The warmth of happiness
To
The dark depths of gloom
I have taken that step
So often on my journey
Walking in circles
Always
Round
And round
And round